Crabs

This book has been reviewed
for accuracy by
David Skryja
Associate Professor of Biology
University of Wisconsin Center—Waukesha.

Library of Congress Cataloging in Publication Data

Pohl, Kathleen.
  Crabs.

  (Nature close-ups)
  Adaptation of: Sawagani / Jun Nanao, Hidetomo
Oda.
  Summary: Discusses the life cycle and behavior
patterns of freshwater crabs.
  1. Crabs—Juvenile literature. 2. Freshwater
invertebrates—Juvenile literature. [1. Crabs]
I. Nanao, Jun. Sawagani. II. Title.
QL444.M33P587 1986   595.3'842   86-26271

ISBN 0-8172-2716-4 (lib. bdg.)
ISBN 0-8172-2734-2 (softcover)

This edition first published in 1987 by Raintree Publishers Inc.

Text copyright © 1987 by Raintree Publishers Inc., translated by Jun
Amano from *Crabs in the Stream* copyright © 1975 by Jun Nanao and
Hidetomo Oda.

Photographs copyright © 1975 by Atsushi Sakurai.

World English translation rights for *Color Photo Books on Nature*
arranged with Kaisei-Sha through Japan Foreign-Rights Center.

1 2 3 4 5 6 7 8 9 0   90 89 88 87 86

Crabs

Adapted by
Kathleen Pohl

Raintree Publishers
Milwaukee

◀ **A mountain stream where crabs live.**

All crabs lived in the ocean at one time. But through the centuries, some species have evolved into freshwater crabs, others into land crabs.

▶ **A freshwater crab that lives in a mountain stream.**

Land crabs return to the ocean to lay their eggs. But freshwater crabs lay their eggs in rivers, ponds, and mountain streams, wherever they happen to live.

There are many different kinds of crabs. In fact, there are more than 4,500 species in all. Many live in deep ocean waters. Others make their homes on sandy beaches. Some live inland but return to the ocean to lay their eggs. But the crabs discussed in this book are freshwater crabs. They live in lakes and marshes, in irrigation ditches and rivers, by waterfalls and in fast-flowing mountain streams.

Crabs belong to a large class of animals which scientists call crustaceans. Crustaceans are animals whose bodies are protected by hard shells. There are more than 30,000 kinds of crustaceans in the world. Lobsters, shrimp, and crayfish are also crustaceans. In many parts of the world, people eat various crustaceans, including some kinds of crabs.

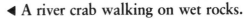

◀ **A river crab walking on wet rocks.**

Crabs have four pairs of walking legs, which help them keep their balance even on wet and slippery rocks. Freshwater crabs can remain out of water as long as their gills stay moist.

Like many crustaceans, crabs breathe through gills. Freshwater crabs can remain out of water for some time, as long as there is enough moisture in the air for them to breathe. If a riverbed dries up, crabs may burrow into the riverbank. Or they may find new homes beneath tree roots or under rocks and stones.

Crabs can see in many directions at once. They have eyes that extend from their bodies on long eyestalks. When crabs are in danger, they can lower their eyestalks into sockets to protect them. Crabs have compound eyes. That means they are made up of thousands of tiny lenses. The eyes detect movement and may also respond to color and light.

Crabs can raise and lower their eyestalks.

compound eyes

socket

Eyestalks raised.

Eyestalks lowered.

◀ **Two crabs fighting over a hiding place.**

The crab's short, squat body easily fits into crevices in rocks or beneath stones. When one crab comes near another's hiding place, the two may fight.

▶ **River crabs searching for food.**

As they crawl about looking for food, these river crabs move sideways, rather than forwards or backwards. The four walking legs on one side of the crab's body push it one way, while the four legs on the other side pull it in the same direction.

All crabs have the same basic body structure. Their short, squat bodies are covered by a hard shell, called an exoskeleton. This acts like a suit of armor to protect the soft, inner body tissues. A special shield, called the carapace, protects the crab's head and midsection, or thorax. Most crabs keep the back part of their body, the abdomen, tucked under them.

All crabs have ten pairs of legs. Usually the four back pairs are used as walking legs. But in some species, one pair of these may be especially adapted for paddling in the water, or for digging in the sand. In almost all species of crabs, the first pair of legs are large, clawlike pincers. Crabs use these pincers, called chelae, to catch food and to protect themselves.

On rainy days, when their bodies won't dry out, freshwater crabs may come out of the water to search for food. They extend their eyestalks so they can see in all directions. They search for grasshoppers, earthworms, and other insects. Insects move slowly on rainy days, and it is fairly easy for crabs to catch them. They use their chelae to seize their prey and tear it apart.

Most freshwater crabs are omnivorous, which means they eat both plants and animals. There are many foods for them in rivers, lakes, and streams. They feed on water plants, fish eggs, insect larvae, fish, frogs, and decaying plant and animal matter.

Crabs that live in the ocean have a different diet. They eat starfish, sea urchins, shellfish, other crustaceans, worms, and seaweed.

● A river crab catches a caterpillar.

These photos show how the crab uses its pincerlike claws to catch its prey. The wormlike caterpillar does not look at all like an adult moth or butterfly. This larval stage of the insect is the second stage of its development. In all, it must go through four stages to become an adult.

▶ **A river crab which has just caught an earthworm.**

The crab uses its large chelae to catch its prey. The four pairs of walking legs support the crab's body as it seizes its prey and feeds itself.

▶ **A river crab holding a grasshopper.**

Crabs may come out of the water to find food in spring and summer if they cannot find enough food in the pond or river where they live.

Various species of crabs have developed different kinds of chelae, depending on the kinds of foods they eat. Some saltwater crabs have pincers especially designed for opening the shells of clams and snails. Others have chelae that are suitable for scraping algae from rocks, or for snapping at prey as it swims by in the ocean. Some species of land crabs have spoon-shaped chelae. They are especially adapted for scooping up beach sand from which particles of food are sifted out. The crab eats the food and rolls the sand into tiny balls which it discards from its mouth. The river crab in these photos has large chelae designed for catching and holding animal prey.

◄ **A river crab feasting on a wasp larva.**

The crab uses the two parts on each chela to hold the wasp larva as it begins to eat it.

The crab's chelae have two parts. One part does not move, but the other does. This lets the crab open and close the pincer. Both parts may have jagged edges for tearing food apart and for holding it tightly.

The crab has a complex set of appendages, or outer mouthparts. They include a pair of true jaws, or mandibles; two pairs of maxillae; and three pairs of maxillipeds. The maxillae and maxillipeds handle the food and help to tear it into pieces before it enters the crab's mouth. It is only the mandibles that actually chew the food.

Only one part of the chela moves.

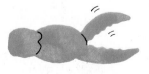

An open chela.

A closed chela.

The female crab eats a lot during spring and summer. Inside her body she carries many eggs, which need a lot of nourishment. Soon she will mate with a male crab. During the mating process, the male gives sperm to the female, which she stores in her body. Later, the sperm join with the eggs, which then become fertilized. From these fertilized eggs, baby crabs will be born.

As the female lays her eggs, they are covered with a kind of gluelike substance. They become attached to her body in a great cluster. The crab carries her eggs in a kind of cradle between her thorax and her up-turned abdomen. She carries them like this until they are ready to hatch.

◀ A river where freshwater crabs live.

▶ A female river crab carrying her eggs.

This mother crab moves slowly and carefully so she will not bump her eggs against the stones. If she senses that anyone is near, she becomes disturbed. Often during this time, crabs remain hidden beneath stones to protect the eggs they are carrying.

◄ A river crab carrying her eggs.

This species of crab lays about forty to fifty eggs at a time. When they are ready to hatch, the mother crab will move to still, shallow water.

► Young crabs developing inside the eggs.

As the young crabs develop, their carapaces and black eyes become visible through the transparent egg cases.

The number of eggs laid by the female depends on the species of crab. Freshwater crabs lay larger and fewer eggs than crabs that lay their eggs in the ocean. A freshwater crab's eggs measure less than one-fifth of an inch in diameter. Tiny crabs' eggs laid in the ocean may be ten times smaller. Saltwater crabs lay from three thousand to three million eggs at a time. Freshwater crabs lay far fewer—perhaps fifty to five hundred eggs in all.

But whether the female crab lays her eggs in the ocean or in fresh water, she carries them cradled in her abdomen until they are ready to hatch. The amount of time varies, depending on the species of crab. The mother crab may carry her eggs for several weeks or many months.

When her eggs are ready to hatch, the freshwater crab moves to the still, shallow waters of the river or lake in which she lives. She shakes her abdomen from side to side. This movement helps to break open the egg cases, and the baby crabs can then work their way out. When the baby crabs come out of, emerge from, the egg cases, they look very much like their parents, except that they are very tiny. The baby crabs cling to their mother for some time before setting out on their own.

But crabs that are born in the ocean do not look at all like their parents at first. The tiny crab larvae must go through several more growth stages before they will resemble adult crabs. The mother crab does not protect the crab larvae. They are left to find food and develop on their own in the ocean. Many crab larvae don't live through this dangerous time in their lives. That is why crabs that lay their eggs in the ocean lay so many eggs.

◄ An egg hatching (photos 1-3).

First, the baby crab sticks its head through the egg case. Then its tiny body emerges. Finally, the crab pulls its long legs out of the egg case. Newly hatched crabs are soft and pale in color.

▼ A newly hatched crab.

Newly hatched freshwater crabs look just like their parents except that they are tiny and color-less. Baby crabs that are born in the ocean look more like shrimp than crabs at first.

◀ **A river crab carrying her babies.**

The mother crab can carry her many babies all at once. But if one falls off, she will not pick it up. She does not feed her young.

The crab's eggs hatch all in one night. The newly emerged fresh-water crabs cling to their mother. They hang onto her small abdominal appendages, which are called swimmerets. By clinging to her, the young crabs are kept from being swept away by strong currents.

The baby crabs stay with their mother for three or four days. During this time, she uses her strong claws to protect them from enemies.

The mother crab shakes her body often to send fresh water over her young. In this way, she makes sure they always have fresh oxygen to breathe.

Swimmerets

Female crabs have swimmerets, to which the baby crabs cling. The swimmerets are covered with hairs.

◀ Baby crabs huddled together on their mother's abdomen.

Baby crabs stay with their mother a few days, until their bodies and legs have hardened. Then they leave, to begin life on their own in the water.

▶ A young crab creeping into a shell.

Baby crabs are not able to defend themselves by fighting because their pincers are not large enough. So sometimes they crawl into shells on the river bottom for protection.

The baby crab's body is soft at first, but within a few days, its exoskeleton hardens. Then it is time for the young crab to begin life on its own in the water. It begins to search for insect larvae to eat. It protects itself by hiding from enemies beneath stones or in empty snail shells. Its pincers are not yet large enough to frighten off enemies.

As the young crab eats and grows larger, its exoskeleton does not grow with it. So, from time to time, crabs, like other crustaceans, must shed, or molt, their shell-like covering. Beneath the old shell is a new and larger shell. Young crabs may molt every couple of weeks. Older crabs molt much less often, perhaps once or twice a year. But all crabs—freshwater, saltwater, and land crabs— molt throughout their lives.

◄ **A snipe preying upon a river crab.**

Birds like snipes and herons often prey upon freshwater crabs. They use their long bills to pluck crabs from their hiding places.

▶ **A river crab which has survived the winter cold.**

This species of crab is full grown when it is a year old. Notice how well the color of its carapace blends with the wet river stones.

Of the many crabs that are born, only a few live to become adults. Freshwater crabs have many enemies, including badgers, weasels, raccoons, turtles, opossums, and birds. But the crab's hard exoskeleton protects it, at least in part, from such predators. And if a crab loses a claw or leg in a battle with another animal, it has the remarkable ability to grow a new one. The crab replaces lost limbs during its next molting. Many crabs, too, have protective coloring. The color of their shells blends in with their surroundings, helping to keep them hidden from enemies.

During the winter, freshwater crabs burrow into the mud at the bottom of lakes and ponds. They do not eat, and their body functions slow way down. But in spring, those crabs which have survived the cold weather become active again. They begin to eat and mate. And so the life cycle of the crab continues.

Let's Find Out

What Kinds of Crabs Live in Rivers?

▶ **Another species of river crab.**

These crabs live at the mouths of rivers. Their long eyestalks are extended as they walk in the shallow water, searching for food.

Molting

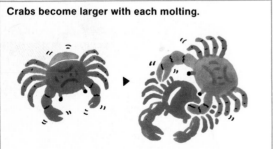

Crabs become larger with each molting.

Some kinds of crabs live at the mouths of rivers or on land most of their lives, but return to the ocean to lay their eggs. The young crab larvae live in the ocean for a while, as they develop into crabs. Then they leave, to begin life on land.

Species of Crabs That Live in Rivers

▲ *Holometopus haematocheir*

These crabs live at the mouths of rivers or on beaches. They have bright red claws and carapaces.

▼ *Sesarma intermedia*

This species of crab can be found on riverbanks or in swamps or wet fields. Their carapaces are about an inch and a half wide.

▼ *Eriocheir japonicus*

These large crabs have very hairy claws. They live upstream in rivers, but return to the ocean to lay their eggs.

▲ *Scopimera globosa*

These crabs live on the beach. They scoop up sand and sift through it to find food to eat. They discard the sand in tiny balls.

▲ *Ilyoplax pusilla*

These tiny crabs live on the beach or at the mouths of rivers. Their carapaces are less than a half inch wide.

▼ *Helice tridens*

The shells of these crabs are bluish in color. The crabs make sounds by rubbing their claws across the edge of their carapaces.

Let's Find Out

What Happens to Crabs That Are Born in the Ocean?

▲ This species of freshwater crab lays forty to fifty eggs at a time. The young crabs are fully developed while they are inside the eggs.

▲ Female red-claw crabs lay about forty thousand eggs at a time. The crab larvae develop in the ocean.

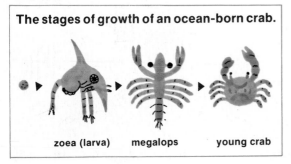

The stages of growth of an ocean-born crab.

zoea (larva)   megalops   young crab

When the crab larvae (zoeae) are born in the ocean, they are no longer protected by the mother crab. They must find food for themselves. As they grow larger and molt, they enter a second stage of development, called megalops. The megalops has huge eyes and looks somewhat like an adult crab. After it grows some more and molts again, a young crab finally emerges.

The Number and Size of the Eggs

Crabs which lay their eggs in the ocean lay many more eggs than freshwater crabs. That is because life in the ocean is very dangerous for the crab larvae. Many are eaten by fish. Freshwater crabs lay less eggs. The mother crab protects the young crabs when they are first born.

◀ **A red-claw crab laying her eggs.**

Female red-claw crabs go to the sea to lay their eggs in fall. When they shake their abdomens, thousands of larvae are hatched from the eggs.

Close-up of a megalops.

A Female and Male River Crab

Male crabs have long, narrow, triangular abdomens. Females have wide, semi-circular abdomens. Their abdomens are larger so they can carry their eggs.

A male crab's abdomen.

A female crab's abdomen.

A female river crab with her young.

GLOSSARY

carapace—the protective shield that covers the crab's head and midsection, or thorax. (pp. 8, 19, 29)

chelae—a crab's large, clawlike pincers. (pp. 8, 12)

compound eyes—eyes comprised of many tiny lenses. (p. 7)

crustaceans—a large class of animals whose bodies are covered with a hard shell-like covering called an exoskeleton. (pp. 4, 11)

eyestalks—the long movable stalks on which the crab's eyes extend from its body. (pp. 7, 28)

molting—the process by which crabs shed their old exoskeletons. (pp. 24, 26, 28)

omnivorous—a word used to describe animals that eat both plants and animals. (p. 11)

predators—animals that hunt and kill other animals for food. (p. 26)

species—a group of animals which scientists have identified as having common traits. (pp. 4, 8, 12)

swimmerets—small appendages on the underside of the female crab's abdomen used for carrying her babies. (p. 23)